YOUNG, GIFTED AND BLACK

WIDE EYED EDITIONS

WELCOME TO THIS BOOK!

Our lives matter. This book is a love letter to our ancestors and to the next generation of black changemakers, in the spirit of the song "To Be Young, Gifted and Black."

The iconic song was written by one of the musicians in this book, Nina Simone. She dedicated it to her friend, Lorraine Hansberry—the first black woman to write a Broadway play. She wrote the song as a tribute to Lorraine's speech *"The Nation Needs Your Gifts,"* which she gave to young black creative writers.

When I first started writing, I was unsure about sharing my stories publicly. My late grandfather, who was born in 1911 and grew up in a segregated community, came to me in a dream. He said: "Go to New York. Write. Write the books you needed when you were younger." He saw what I could be, before I could understand the depth of my potential.

For Andrea, the experience of illustrating this book while expecting a baby boy crystallized the importance of books that show people who look like him. We wish for every child who encounters *Young, Gifted and Black* to know that the world needs your "gifts," that they are more than enough, and that we see your greatness today, tomorrow, and beyond.

We both believe in the power of creating what we need to see. The books we read and the media we consume deeply influence our understanding of who we are and what we can be—if you can't see it you can't be it. They also impact how we understand each other. And although a lot has changed since Lorraine's speech and Nina's song were written, the stories in movies, in school, and on television often show a limited view of the achievements and stories of people of color.

All children deserve to see themselves represented positively in stories. That's why we're highlighting the talent and contributions of black changemakers from around the world—for readers of all backgrounds to discover.

This book is a beginning and not an end. We're inviting you on a journey through time, across borders, and even through space (with astronaut Mae Jemison!) that provides a small but mighty snapshot of the infinite amount of celebrated and unsung heroes worldwide, including yourselves and the people you care about.

Let's look to the lessons of the past while imagining what's possible when we dare to be bold. While each of the 52 visionary leaders we've highlighted has unique strengths and have endured various heartbreaks and triumphs, they share their fearless pursuit of the dreams they had as a child.

We hope that you're just as encouraged by the artists, activists, doers, makers, healers, and dreamers who bravely paved the way for us to have a brighter future.

Jamia Wilson & Andrea Pippins

JAMIA WILSON

ANDREA PIPPINS

Mary Seacole

NOV. 23, 1805 – MAY 14, 1881
KINGSTON, JAMAICA

Heroine of the Crimean War, Mary Seacole, pioneered as a NURSE who cared for British soldiers at the battlefront.

As a child, young Mary learned about Caribbean medicine from her mother, a free black Jamaican woman. A natural healer, she practiced nursing dolls and pets before tending to humans.

By 1854, Mary was living in London when the suffering of soldiers in the Crimean War went public. At the start of the war, her application to join Florence Nightingale's nursing team was rejected—like many others who were refused due to their race or class. Determined to help, Mary put her nursing skills to use and went to war at her own expense.

In 1855, she built the British Hotel near Balaklava to care for injured soldiers. She helped contain the cholera outbreak by distributing remedies in hospitals on the Crimean frontlines.

Although she passed away in 1881, *"Mother Seacole"* is remembered for bravely running a business, kindly caring for ill and injured warriors, and defying discrimination during an era when black women's rights were limited.

MATTHEW HENSON

AUGUST 8, 1866 – MARCH 9, 1955 · NANJEMOY, MARYLAND · USA

Matthew Alexander Henson was the first African-American Arctic EXPLORER. He made six exploration voyages over the course of 18 years.

Born to poor tenant farmers who passed away during his childhood, Matthew became a dishwasher at Janey's Home-Cooked Meals Café to support himself when he was about eleven years old. One of his favorite parts of the work was learning about the customers' lives. He was especially fascinated by sailors and any interesting voyages.

Aged 12, he walked forty miles from his home to Baltimore to work on a merchant boat. Once he was hired, he learned how to read and write from the ship's captain. Always adventurous, Matthew sailed all around the world.

In 1890, he joined voyager Robert Peary's first Arctic expedition across the northern tip of Greenland. He went on to cover almost 10,000 miles on dogsleds across Greenland and Canada.

Matthew's team made history by becoming the first explorers to reach the North Pole in 1909. Matthew declared, *"I think I'm the first man to sit on top of the world."*

AVA DUVERNAY

AUGUST 24, 1972
LONG BEACH, CALIFORNIA
USA

Ava DuVernay was the first black female **FILM DIRECTOR** to win a Golden Globe Award, and the first African American to win Best Director at the 2012 Sundance Film Festival.

As a child, Ava grew up near Compton, a mostly black and Latino city in southern Los Angeles County. Throughout the school year, she attended an all-girls Catholic school, and discovered her love of movies while watching films with her Aunt Denise.

Ava often visited her father's childhood home in Hayneville, Alabama during summer vacations. Later, Ava said that trips to her father's hometown inspired her Oscar nominated film *Selma*, about marches for voter equality in the 1960s.

As a publicist turned filmmaker, Ava attributes her success to creativity and determination. She advises aspiring directors to: *"Be passionate and move forward with gusto every single hour of every single day until you reach your goal."*

PILOT LICENSE

BESSIE COLEMAN

JANUARY 26, 1892 – APRIL 30, 1926
ATLANTA, TEXAS · USA

Bessie Coleman was an **AIRSHOW PILOT**, and the first African American and Native American to stage a public flight.

One of 13 kids, Bessie trekked for four hours a day to her one-room school in Texas. Always a high flyer, she excelled at mathematics and reading. When she wasn't studying, she helped out on her family farm and attended church. Her determination and drive led to her gaining a place at Langston University in Oklahoma. But college fees were expensive, and Bessie had to leave after completing only one semester.

Aged 23, Bessie heard stories from World War One pilots during her job as a manicurist. Their adventures inspired her. Since U.S. flight schools denied women and blacks entry, Bessie became a licensed pilot in France. Although a crash ended the aviator's dream of opening a school for black fliers, her legacy continues. Mae Jemison, the first black female astronaut in space, brought a photo of *"Brave Bessie"* on her first mission.

BARACK OBAMA
AUGUST 4, 1961
HONOLULU, HAWAII · USA

MICHELLE OBAMA
JANUARY 17, 1964
CHICAGO, ILLINOIS · USA

Barack Hussein Obama served as the **44TH PRESIDENT OF THE UNITED STATES OF AMERICA**. He was the nation's first African-American president.

Barack Obama was born to a Kenyan economist and an American anthropologist in Honolulu, Hawaii. He spent his childhood attending school and playing basketball in Hawaii and Indonesia. His experiences growing up in Catholic and Muslim schools expanded his worldview. He said, *"I benefited from a multiplicity of cultures that all fed me."*

Barack studied at Occidental College, Columbia University. After graduation, he went on to work as a community organizer in Chicago before enrolling at Harvard Law School. After this, he worked as a civil rights lawyer and professor, penned *Dreams of My Father*, a personal story about race and identity, and served as a Senator in Illinois.

His commitment to public service and grassroots organizing secured his two election victories as president.

Michelle Obama is a **LAWYER** who served as the **44TH FIRST LADY OF THE UNITED STATES** (FLOTUS). She pioneered as the first African-American FLOTUS.

Michelle LaVaughn Robinson was born and raised in Chicago's South Side. She lived in a tiny bungalow with her parents and her older brother. As a part of a supportive family who valued reading and education, both Michelle and her brother moved forward a grade at school.

Her academic excellence brought her to Chicago's first magnet school for gifted kids, where she graduated as salutatorian. She went on to study at Princeton University and Harvard Law School. She said *"For me, education was power."*

Michelle worked as a lawyer, city administrator, and a community outreach professional. As First Lady, she became known as a riveting public speaker, fashion icon, and advocate for military families, health, and wellness causes.

Barack and Michelle Obama have been married since 1992 and have two daughters called Malia and Sasha.

CHIMAMANDA NGOZI ADICHIE

september 15, 1977 · ENUGU, NIGERIA

Chimamanda Ngozi Adichie is a MacArthur Genius Grant AWARD WINNING AUTHOR. Her writing has been translated into 30 languages.

Chimamanda grew up in Enugu, southeast Nigeria, as one of six children. Her father was a statistics professor and her mother was the University of Nigeria's first woman registrar. Chimamanda began reading when she was four, and started writing as soon as she could spell.

The majority of the books she read in her early life focused on British and American characters, who didn't reflect her reality in Nigeria. Although these books influenced her early writing, she says her discovery of African authors helped her *"Realize that people who looked like me could live in books."* This inspired her to amplify her distinct cultural voice.

Famous for her lectures and writing about gender equality and the value of diverse storytelling, the author of *We Should All Be Feminists* and *Americanah*, opens minds one story at a time.

CATHY FREEMAN

FEBRUARY 16, 1973
SLADE POINT, MACKAY · AUSTRALIA

As the sixth fastest woman of all time, Cathy Freeman made headlines for being a CHAMPION SPRINTER.

When Cathy Freeman's family noticed her running talent, her mother urged her to develop her skill. A member of the Kuku Yalanji people, Cathy faced hardship due to economic instability and racial discrimination. In primary school, she was denied medals that were given to white girls even when she surpassed them on the field.

Despite roadblocks, she persisted: *"You got to try and reach for the stars or try and achieve the unreachable."* A scholarship positioned her to compete at the National School Championships. This paved the way for wins in the Australian National Championships and the World Junior Games.

Cathy made history as the first indigenous Australian to compete in the Olympics. Her trailblazing activity raised awareness about issues impacting indigenous people. When she won the Olympic gold medal in 2000, she ran her victory lap barefoot as a tribute to her heritage.

George Washington Carver

1863 or 1864 – JANUARY 5, 1943
DIAMOND, MISSOURI · USA

Known as "the plant doctor," SCIENTIST George Washington Carver devised over 100 products using peanuts as his only crop.

George Washington Carver was born into slavery in Diamond Grove, Missouri during the Civil War. At one week old, he was kidnapped by outlaws. He eventually returned to his birthplace towards the end of the war.

George was a sickly child, so he focused on household chores and gardening. When slavery was abolished, he learned to read and write from the family that formerly enslaved him.

After being rejected from college due to discrimination, he studied art, piano, and botany in Iowa. He went on to become the first black student and teacher at Iowa State College.

George's success led him to direct the department of agriculture at the Tuskegee Institute. His findings and inventions helped poor cotton farmers adapt their crops and improve their health. *Time* magazine called him *"Black Leonardo,"* in reference to the Italian artist and inventor Leonardo da Vinci, for his ground-breaking agricultural artistry.

MALORIE BLACKMAN
FEBRUARY 8, 1962
LONDON, ENGLAND
UNITED KINGDOM

Renowned AUTHOR of more than 60 books, including the Noughts and Crosses series, Malorie Blackman was the U.K.'s Children's Laureate.

The daughter of Bajan parents, Malorie Blackman was born in London. A lover of literature, she read all of the children's books in her local library by age 11, including one of her favorite texts, C.S. Lewis' *The Silver Chair*.

Aged 28, Malorie published her first book, *Not So Stupid*, after working as a systems programmer. Before she found a publisher, her manuscript was rejected over 80 times.

Her persistence drove her success as a prolific writer, and she became an Officer of the Order of the British Empire and the UK's first black Children's Laureate. During her tenure, she said, *"Reading is an exercise in empathy; an exercise in walking in someone else's shoes for a while."*

Harriet Tubman

1822 – MARCH 10, 1913
DORCHESTER COUNTY, MARYLAND · USA

Nicknamed Moses, Harriet Tubman led hundreds of slaves to freedom as one of the most notorious CONDUCTORS on the Underground Railroad.

Harriet Tubman was born a slave in Maryland. She worked as a house servant from age five onwards. Aged 12, she was forced to labor in the fields. Then, she was struck by an overseer for defending another slave, sustaining a head injury which resulted in lifelong visions and vivid dreams.

In 1849, Harriet ran away in fear of being sold. By following the North Star, she traveled to Philadelphia. Her escape inspired her to rescue her family and many others. She made the risky trip south 19 times, using the Underground Railroad, a network of safe houses and allies.

Harriet, who was also an advocate for women's rights, said she *"Never lost a single passenger"* when she spoke about the 300 slaves she escorted to freedom.

MO FARAH

MARCH 23, 1983
MOGADISHU, SOMALIA

Mo Farah is one of England's greatest athletes. The LONG-DISTANCE RUNNER was knighted after winning two gold medals at the 2016 Rio Olympics.

Although Mo was born in Somalia, he lived with his grandmother and his twin brother in Djibouti before moving to England. Without knowing English upon his arrival in the UK, the eight-year-old soccer fan had to adjust to both a new school and culture without his twin by his side.

Although he dreamed of playing football for Arsenal as a child, Mo focused on track and field due to his stamina and speed. He developed his running skills in high school, where he began training with support from his physical education teacher.

Ever since he won the English schools cross-country championship at fifteen, Mo has been blazing trails and breaking records worldwide. The Olympian credits *"Honesty, fairness, and friendship"* as traits that help drive his success.

JEAN-MICHEL BASQUIAT

DECEMBER 22, 1960 – AUGUST 12, 1988 · BROOKLYN, NEW YORK · USA

American **PAINTER** Jean-Michel Basquiat was a street artist and expressive painter who collaborated with pop artist Andy Warhol.

The son of a Puerto Rican mother and a Haitian father, Jean-Michel Basquiat joined the Brooklyn Museum as a junior member at six-years-old. Fluent in French, English, and Spanish by age 11, Jean-Michel dreamed of becoming a cartoonist. After surviving a car accident, his mother gave him a copy of the medical book *Gray's Anatomy*. He became fascinated with the structure of the human body and often referenced it in his art. He made poetry, music, and street art in high school, practicing learning by doing: *"I start a picture and I finish it."*

After his graffiti tag became famous, he caught the attention of the art world. His paintings gained recognition throughout his twenties. Basquiat's imaginative mix of "high art" with pop culture—and his references to jazz, hip hop, and black history—catapulted him to celebrity. When he died, he left behind over 1,000 unseen paintings.

JESSE ★OWENS

SEPTEMBER 12, 1913 – MARCH 31, 1980
OAKVILLE, ALABAMA · USA

Once known as the fastest man in the world, Olympic TRACK AND FIELD CHAMPION Jesse Owens won four gold medals at the 1936 Berlin Games.

James Cleveland Owens was a frail child whose condition sometimes prevented him from helping his family with farm work. When he was eight, they moved from Alabama to Ohio for better opportunities. When a teacher wrote his initials 'J. C.' as 'Jesse' by mistake, he decided to keep it.

By fifth grade, Jesse grew into a strong runner and joined the track team. After setting records in the 100 and 200-yard dash, and the broad jump, his coach described him as appearing to float in air.

Jesse's success attracted college recruiters. By this time, Jesse was a young father, and so attended Ohio State University (O.S.U.) to stay near family. Jesse reigned as O.S.U.'s first black sports team captain. Nicknamed the *"Buckeye Bullet,"* he set three world records and made history as an Olympic champion.

BEYONCÉ

September 4, 1981
HOUSTON, TEXAS
USA ★

Beyoncé Knowles is a multi-platinum, Grammy Award-winning POP SINGER known for her dynamic vocals, iconic style, and dramatic video and live performances.

Although the Knowles sisters are both uniquely talented, they have their trendsetting glamour, dedication to social causes, and powerful storytelling in common.

Born to a salon owner and a businessman, Beyoncé was the first of two daughters. The talented Texan learned to dance, and won a competition with her performance of John Lennon's "Imagine" at St. Mary's Elementary School.

At eight, she joined Girl's Tyme, a five-girl act managed by her father. Although the group was defeated on a TV talent show, they persisted. This led to their transformation into Destiny's Child, which launched them into stardom.

The force behind the ensemble, Beyoncé rose to fame. Ever since her solo debut topped the charts in 2003, the woman who described herself as an *"Introverted kid who broke out of her shell on stage"* has remained an icon. "Lemonade" was her sixth album to hit number one.

SOLANGE

June 24, 1986
HOUSTON, TEXAS
USA

Solange Knowles is a Grammy Award-winning songwriter, model, actress, social justice advocate, and SOUL-SINGING SUPERSTAR.

Solange, Beyoncé's younger sister, refers to the women who visited her mother's hair salon as her "2000 aunties." She credits their influence with sparking her passion for storytelling and supporting women and girls.

The skilful songwriter won second place in a notable jingle-writing competition in elementary school. In her teens, she performed as a backup dancer for Destiny's Child and made her professional vocal debut on the group's 2001 holiday album.

Solange also built systems of support for other black girls in her mostly white private school. She started "The BF Club" to *"Create a fellowship in a space that felt like it didn't belong to us"* long before her Grammy-winning album, "A Seat at the Table," called for self-definition, cultural pride, and co-operative action in 2016.

KATHERINE JOHNSON

AUGUST 26, 1918
WHITE SULPHUR SPRINGS
WEST VIRGINIA · USA

PHYSICIST and **MATHEMATICIAN** Katherine Johnson calculated the flight path for the first American mission to space.

Katherine always loved counting. She liked the certainty of math because *"You're either right or you're wrong."* Starting high school at 10, and college at 15, her appetite for learning helped her blaze through courses.

Despite her dream of becoming a mathematician, she believed her options were limited to "being a nurse or a teacher" due to barriers to equal education and employment. Nonetheless, Katherine focused on geometry, the study of lines, shapes, and angles, throughout university.

Her determination paved her way to NASA (National Aeronautics and Space Administration). There, she calculated pathways for spacecrafts to orbit Earth and land on the moon. Her work opened doors for women and African Americans in the fields of mathematics and computing.

In 2015, she received the Presidential Medal of Freedom, the highest civilian award in the U.S.A.

Josephine Baker

JUNE 3, 1906 – APRIL 12, 1975
ST. LOUIS, MISSOURI • USA

Josephine Baker was an American-born French ENTERTAINER, World War Two resistance SPY, and a CIVIL RIGHTS ACTIVIST.

The daughter of a laundress and a drummer, Josephine grew up in poverty. Forced to work as a servant to provide food for her family, she took on adult responsibilities when she was eight.

By 13, Josephine ran away from home. When she wasn't working, she performed on street corners. Her talent landed her a job dancing, singing, and acting for local vaudeville shows.

Several years later, she made her Broadway debut in the musical "Shuffle Along." Her success propelled her to France in 1925, where she captured the hearts of audiences. Within a decade, Josephine became one of the most well-known stars in Europe after dancing in a banana skirt during her iconic show, *"La Folie du Jour."* When World War Two broke out, she helped support the allies by working as a spy. While she toured Europe, she passed on secret messages that were hidden in her sheet music. After the war, she went on to adopt 12 children.

KOFI ANNAN

APRIL 8, 1938
KUMASI, GHANA

Knowledge is Power

Ghanaian **DIPLOMAT** Kofi Annan is the former Secretary-General of the United Nations and a recipient of the Nobel Peace Prize.

Kofi and his twin sister were born to an aristocratic family in Ghana, which was then known as the Gold Coast. He attended a Christian boarding school until his graduation in 1957, the year Ghana became the first British African colony to claim independence.

Fueled by his passion for education and his belief that *"Knowledge is power, information is liberating,"* Kofi studied at four colleges in Ghana, Switzerland, and the United States.

In 1962, he became a staff member at the United Nations where he eventually became the U.N. Secretary-General and a special envoy to Syria. Kofi and the United Nations were jointly awarded the Nobel Peace Prize in 2001 "for their work for a better organized and more peaceful world."

Langston Hughes

FEB. 1, 1902 – MAY 22, 1967
JOPLIN, MISSOURI · USA

Langston Hughes is one of the most well-known WRITERS of the Harlem Renaissance—an artistic movement that took place after World War One.

Langston was raised by his grandmother in Lawrence, Kansas. When she passed away, Langston moved to Illinois, and then Ohio to live with his mother. In Illinois, the talented young writer was elected class poet by his schoolmates.

Inspired by writers Carl Sandburg and Walt Whitman, he contributed to his high school's literary magazine and yearbook.

Following graduation, Langston lived in Mexico for a year with his father. During this time, he published "The Negro Speaks of Rivers" in *The Crisis* magazine. The lyrical traveler served as a steward on a ship from Africa to Spain, and later published poetry in Paris.

The man who wrote *"Hold fast to dreams, for if dreams die, life is a broken-winged bird that cannot fly,"* took his own advice and became a prolific writer despite hardship. After releasing his first book of poetry in 1926, he penned over 60 books including memoirs, novels, musicals, opera, children's poetry, short stories, and plays.

TONI MORRISON

FEBRUARY 18, 1931
LORAIN, OHIO · USA

NOVELIST Toni Morrison was the first African-American woman to receive the Nobel Prize in literature.

Toni was born to a working class family in Ohio. Her parents inspired her interest in music, reading, and folklore.

She grew up in a mixed neighborhood, and said she didn't develop a full understanding of racism until her teen years. She said, *"When I was in first grade, nobody thought I was inferior. I was the only black in the class and the only child who could read."*

Studious and driven, Toni graduated with honors. She moved to Washington, D.C. to study at Howard University, and later Cornell University in New York. Later, Toni became a professor and published her first novel, *The Bluest Eye*.

Toni's dedication to her craft led to her winning the Pulitzer Prize, the Nobel Prize, and the Presidential Medal of Freedom.

BRIAN LARA ★

MAY 2, 1969
SANTA CRUZ, TRINIDAD AND TOBAGO

World renowned **CRICKETER** and record-breaker Brian Lara is widely regarded as one of the greatest batsmen of all time.

The 10th of 11 children, Brian began playing cricket at the Harvard Coaching Clinic when he was six years old. His early education on correct batting technique helped him make Trinidad's under-16 team.

By the time Brian was 20, he became Trinidad and Tobago's youngest captain. Brian made headlines for breaking two cricket batting records in 1994, and for becoming the sport's most prolific scorer in 2005. He said, *"Like most sportsmen, I am very nervous before I go on to bat. If someone is not nervous, I am not sure what sport they are involved in."*

Today, the left-handed match-winner holds the record for the highest individual score in first-class cricket. Now a sports and tourism ambassador, Brian has traded his bat for a golf club. He participates in celebrity golf tournaments worldwide.

MADAM C.J. WALKER

(SARAH BREEDLOVE) DECEMBER 23, 1867 – MAY 25, 1919
DELTA, LOUISIANA · USA

Madam C.J. Walker was the first black female MILLIONAIRE. She invented a line of best-selling African-American hair products.

Madam C.J. Walker was born Sarah Breedlove on the plantation where her parents had been enslaved during the Civil War. After losing both her parents at seven years old, she moved to Mississippi with her sister, Louvenia, to build a better future.

In 1906, Sarah married C.J. Walker and took his name. When a common scalp condition led to hair loss, she developed a homemade treatment that she began selling to other black women with the same ailment.

Walker went on to build a beauty empire. She placed adverts with photos of her own "before and after" shots in African-American newspapers, sold her products in churches, and trained others to share stories about the Madam C.J. Walker lifestyle.

Known for saying *"I got my start by giving myself a start,"* Walker paved the way for others to live their dreams. She created jobs for women, and supported educational scholarships and charities. She also traveled to the White House to urge President Wilson to end racial violence.

YANNICK NOAH

MAY 18, 1960
SEDAN, FRANCE

Yannick Noah is a French TENNIS CHAMPION. He is best known for his 1983 French Open win.

The son of a French mother and Cameroonian father, Yannick followed in the sporting footsteps of his dad, a professional footballer. During his childhood, Yannick devoted his time to training on the tennis court and even made his own tennis racket to practice with. His efforts paid off and caught the attention of tennis legend Arthur Ashe.

While training, he had to spend months away from his family, so Yannick turned to music to help with his loneliness. He said, *"When one sings, one does not speak about the problems of the every day. One speaks about the things which inspire us."*

By the age of 17, Yannick had won Wimbledon's junior category. He went on to achieve victories including the French Junior, Italian Open, and Benson and Hedges titles with his signature flamboyant style.

Today, Yannick's legacy continues through his charity for children, and his son, basketballer Joakim Noah. Now, he remains the only French athlete to successfully become a popstar after retirement.

MAURICE ASHLEY

MARCH 6, 1966
ST. ANDREW, JAMAICA

Maurice Ashley made history as the first African-American CHESS GRANDMASTER in the world. He is also an author, commentator, and puzzle inventor.

As a child, Maurice Ashley learned about chess from watching his brother and his friends play in and around the city of Kingston, Jamaica. Aged 12, he left his birthplace to move to New York City.

Throughout high school, he developed his skill and focus in Brooklyn's parks and chess clubs. Maurice continued to play in chess tournaments, winning game after game. He became the first African-American international grandmaster, which is the highest title that can be awarded in chess.

Today, the chess grandmaster and puzzle inventor is a commentator for the world's most well-known chess tournaments. He is also a coach to kids in Harlem, encouraging and promoting the game among young people there. Connecting his rise from the inner-city streets to the U.S. Chess Hall of Fame, he declared, *"All those roses growing from concrete, just want a chance to live their passion and be great."*

ALEXANDRE DUMAS
JULY 24, 1802 – DEC. 5, 1870
VILLERS-COTTERÊTS, FRANCE

Alexandre Dumas is the famed AUTHOR of *The Count of Monte Cristo* and *The Three Musketeers*, which have been translated into over 100 languages.

Known for his historical adventure novels, French author and playwright Alexandre was born Dumas Davy de la Pailleterie in 1802.

During his childhood, he lived in Viller-Cotterêts with his mother, Marie Louise and father, Thomas-Alexandre. His father was the highest ranking black man in a European army at that time.

Aged 20, he moved to the city of Paris to scribe for King Louis Phillippe. There, he occupied himself with Romantic drama and comedic storytelling. Due to the popularity of his writing, Dumas was able to build his prized castle, the Château de Monte-Cristo.

Sadly, his fortune transformed into debt in 1851, which forced him into exile. At the end of his life, the writer who famously coined *"All for one, and one for all"* had published over 100,000 pages of work.

I HAVE A DREAM

One of the most influential leaders in U.S. history, Martin Luther King, Jr. was a **CIVIL RIGHTS ACTIVIST** who devoted his life to advancing racial equality.

Martin Luther King, Jr. was a dreamer who turned his vision into action. Long before he became famous for his epic speeches, he envisaged a world where *"Children will live in a nation where they will not be judged by the color of their skin, but the content of their character."*

The son of a preacher, Martin, who was born Michael, moved forward two grades at high school, which earned him admission to the prestigious Morehouse University at age 15. Inspired by his religious father, he later earned a doctorate in divinity.

In 1955, he became the spokesperson for the Montgomery Bus Boycott, a campaign to stop segregation on city buses. He increased support for civil rights by organising peaceful protests.

Martin helped organize the March on Washington for Jobs and Freedom in 1963, and delivered his famous "I Have a Dream" speech. A year later, United States Congress passed the Civil Rights Act outlawing segregation.

In 1964, Martin won the Nobel Peace Prize, and helped pass the Voting Rights Act. Although he didn't get to live to see his dream of racial and economic equality for all people realized, the man who said, "only in the darkness can you see the stars" created a brighter future for generations to come.

Today, Martin Luther King Day is a federal holiday in the U.S. observed on the third Monday of January each year.

MAYA ANGELOU

APRIL 4, 1928 – MAY 28, 2014
ST. LOUIS, MISSOURI · USA

Celebrated for her poetry, essays, screenplays, and acting, Maya Angelou was a **WRITER** and **CIVIL RIGHTS ACTIVIST**.

Before Maya Angelou became a household name, she had a difficult childhood. After her parents separated, Maya and her brother traveled by themselves to live in Stamps, Arkansas with their grandmother. But there, her uncle taught her to read, which inspired her passion for books.

At seven, Maya was attacked by her mother's boyfriend. Her distress caused her to stop speaking for years. Later, she based her autobiography, *I Know Why the Caged Bird Sings*, on this experience.

As an adult, Maya became San Francisco's first black female cable car conductor and the first African-American woman to have her screenplay produced.

The author of seven memoirs fought for equal rights for women and African Americans throughout her life. She said, *"You alone are enough. You have nothing to prove to anybody."*

NINA SIMONE

FEBRUARY 21, 1933 – APRIL 21, 2003
TRYON, NORTH CAROLINA
USA

Known for her honest lyrics and fiery performances, SINGER, PIANIST, and CIVIL RIGHTS ACTIVIST Nina Simone broke cultural barriers.

At three, Nina began playing piano before she could reach the pedals. A lonely child, she took comfort in connecting with others through music.

Nina trained to become a classical pianist from age six onwards. At 12, her recital was interrupted by the discord of discrimination. When Nina's parents were removed from their seats, she demanded their return to the front row.

Her community believed in her gifts and helped fundraise for her education at the Julliard School of Music. When her money ran out, she played jazz at clubs to support herself. She gained a following, and in 1957, her Top 20 track "I Loves You Porgy" introduced her to the world stage.

Nina also used her voice as a megaphone for the civil rights movement in the sixties. She said, *"There's no excuse for young people not knowing who the heroes and heroines were."* Enraged by racial injustice in the U.S., she lived abroad from 1973 until her death.

SIMONE BILES

MARCH 14, 1997
COLUMBUS, OHIO·USA

GOLD

GOLD

Earning more Olympic and World Championship medals than any other American GYMNAST, Simone Biles led the U.S. Olympic women's gymnastics team to victory in 2016.

Simone Biles was flying high long before she defied gravity as the most decorated female gymnast in America. From competing with her brothers on the trampoline, to climbing a four-foot mailbox and teaching herself how to do back tucks, her adventurous spirit defined her early on.

Raised in Texas, Simone and her siblings were placed in foster care because their birth mother was unable to care for them. Her grandparents adopted her and her younger sister, providing them with a safe and supportive home.

After six-year-old Simone's natural talent caught the attention of a local gym coach, she began training. She developed her strength, practiced with her sister, and observed Olympian regimens to sharpen her skills.

Although Simone's drive helped her turn challenges into Olympic gold, her demanding schedule forced her to miss high school football games and dances. Despite this, her unmatched tumbling, flipping, and floor exercise skills paid off. She became the first woman gymnast since 1974 to win four consecutive all-around titles at the U.S. National Gymnastics Championships, and the first female ever to be the all-around world champion three years in a row. Of her experience, she said: *"Making history is cool."*

Simone, the shortest of all of the 555 American athletes at the 2016 Olympics, rises above the rest in life and sport. She made headlines for saying, "smiling doesn't win gold medals" when a *Dancing with the Stars* host criticized her for not smiling enough during her flawless routine.

STEVIE Wonder

MAY 13, 1950 • SAGINAW, MICHIGAN • U.S.A.

Stevie Wonder is an award-winning MUSICIAN, former child prodigy, and pop-culture legend.

The third of six children, Steveland Judkins Hardaway Morris was born a preemie in Saginaw, Michigan. As a result of being born early, he lost his ability to see.

Aged 11, Steveland signed a contract with the hit-making Motown record company. Two years later, the boy, now known by his stage name Little Stevie Wonder, topped the charts with his song "Fingertips." This was the first live recording to have this honor, and the first single to lead the Billboard and R&B charts at the same time.

A prodigy, Stevie dazzled global audiences with his expert harmonica, piano, drums, and vocal skills. As he came of age, his voice changed along with his body. This almost resulted in him being dropped from Motown, which caused him to abandon the "Little" nickname and develop his identity as Stevie Wonder, the grown-up vocalist.

In the absence of sight, Stevie uses his voice to share the hope he envisages for humanity. He said, *"Just because a man lacks the use of his eyes doesn't mean he lacks vision."*

As one of the 60 best-selling artists worldwide, the 25 time Grammy Award winner uses his popularity to champion social causes. Due in part to his support, Dr. Martin Luther King, Jr.'s birthday is now a national holiday in the United States.

ESPERANZA SPALDING

OCTOBER 18, 1984
PORTLAND, OREGON·USA

Esperanza Spalding is a Grammy Award-winning JAZZ BASSIST and SINGER.

Esperanza Spalding was born to a mixed-race single mother in what she described as a "rough neighborhood" in Portland, Oregon. She was a curious child, and her passion for music from different cultures inspired her.

At age four, she discovered cellist Yo-Yo Ma while watching an episode of *Mister Rogers' Neighborhood*. Inspired by Ma, she taught herself to play the violin aged five, and performed with the Chamber Music Society of Oregon until she was 15.

Esperanza attended the Northwest Academy on scholarship and studied the oboe and clarinet. In high school, she shifted her attention to the upright bass and started songwriting for a local rock band.

While at the Berklee School of Music, she began making waves with her unique ability to write music, sing in three languages, and play bass. She credits her exceptional style to her diverse influences, *"If you're a writer, and you write fiction, that's not all you read."*

Her openness to diverse influences sculpted her sound and helped her win the Best New Artist Grammy Award in 2011.

Acclaimed FILMMAKER, ACTOR, and DIRECTOR, Sir Sidney Poitier was the first Bahamian and African-American to win an Academy Award for Best Actor.

Born while his Bahamian parents were vacationing in Florida, Sidney was a preemie. Although he wasn't expected to survive, he grew stronger and moved to his family's tomato farm in the Bahamas.

Sidney's father was worried he would become involved in mischief, so sent him to live with his brother in Miami at 14. But at 16, he moved to New York City after encountering the Ku Klux Klan, a violent hate group.

Making a living in the city was difficult. While working odd jobs, he spotted a flyer about acting opportunities at the American Negro Theatre. Since he couldn't sing or dance like black actors were expected to do at the time, he focused on acting.

Sidney stuck to his motto: *"To simply wake up every morning a better person than when I went to bed."* He went on to become the first African-American to win an Oscar for his performance in *Lilies of the Field*. His acting positively changed portrayals of black people in the media.

SIDNEY POITIER
FEBRUARY 20, 1927
MIAMI, FLORIDA • USA

OPRAH WINFREY

JANUARY 29, 1954
KOSCIUSKO, MISSISSIPPI · USA

Oprah Winfrey is one of the most well-known TALK SHOW HOSTS in the world. She is also a network owner, actress, and producer.

Oprah was born "Orpah" in Mississippi to a teenage single mother. Since her name was often mispronounced, she changed it to "Oprah." She was raised by her grandmother, who taught her to read before she was three.

At six, she went to live with her mother, a housemaid, who was away a lot due to her hectic schedule. Life at home was hard and Oprah ran away. Despite her difficult childhood, Oprah stood out as a talented speaker at school. Her gift for gab earned her a full scholarship to Tennessee State University.

Aged 19, Oprah became Nashville's first black female news anchor. Her success paved the way for her to host the world famous *Oprah Winfrey Show* for twenty-five seasons.

Oprah encouraged her audience to follow her example by *"Turning wounds into wisdom."* Her positive message inspired millions, including President Obama. He awarded her the Presidential Medal of Freedom in 2013.

Pelé (EDSON ARANTES do NASCIMENTO)

OCTOBER 23, 1940
TRÊS CORAÇÕES,
MINAS GERAIS · BRAZIL

Pelé is widely accepted as the greatest SOCCER PLAYER of all time, as a legendary member of three Brazilian World Cup-champion teams.

A shining star from the start, Edson was named after the inventor of the light bulb Thomas Edison. He was born to Dona Celeste and "Dondinho" Ramos before he rose from the slums of Sao Paulo, to become the world's greatest soccer player.

When Edson wasn't in school or working in a tea shop, he practiced soccer with his father—a former striker who retired due to an injury. Since he couldn't afford a ball, he played with grapefruit and socks stuffed with paper and tied with string.

Edson learned "ginga," from his father. Ginga is a style of footwork rooted in "capoeira," the movements African slaves developed in the 16th century to escape captivity. Pelé's father inspired him to join a youth club coached by a former member of Brazil's national team.

Aged 15, Edson tried out for Santos, a professional team. He scored his first goal a year later, which sparked his rise to the national team, where he led Brazil's first World Cup victory at 17.

Edson's motto is *"Everything is practice."* The 1999 FIFA Co-Player of the Century says dedication to the sport helped him achieve three World Cup titles.

Nelson Mandela

July 18, 1918 – December 5, 2013
Mvezo Transkei, South Africa

Nelson Mandela was a Nobel Peace Prize winner and the former **PRESIDENT OF SOUTH AFRICA.**

President Mandela was born on the river banks of a village in South Africa to parents in the Tembu people's royal family. They gave him the name "Rolihlahla," which means "troublemaker" in the Xhosa language, a title that he would live up to for the rest of his life.

Rolihlahla loved learning and said "Education is the most powerful weapon we can use to change the world." He went to a mission school where his teacher started calling him "Nelson."

Nelson was treated cruelly due to apartheid, a system that used laws to discriminate against people based on their skin color. Although they were the majority, blacks had no input into how their country was run and were barred access to education and fair wages. They were also met with violence when they stood up for their rights.

Nelson spoke out about human rights, which caused important people to stop trading with South Africa. He was jailed for 27 years, initially in a small cell in Robben Island prison, for standing up for equality.

Getting into "good trouble" helped Nelson transform his country. Although he had "A Long Walk to Freedom," as his memoir is named, he is celebrated for promoting peace, and building bridges between people. His later work with former President F.W. de Klerk helped end apartheid and steered South Africa's peaceful transition to majority rule when he became president in 1994. He lived by the words *"It always seems impossible until it's done."*

Nelson passed away in 2013, but his legacy of resistance, hope, and dignity lives on in South Africa's emerging "born-free" generation.

LOUIS ARMSTRONG

AUGUST 4, 1901 – JULY 6, 1971
NEW ORLEANS, LOUISIANA
USA

Known as "Satchmo" or "Pops", Louis Armstrong is one of history's most influential ENTERTAINERS. "Satch" is best known for his songs "What a Wonderful World" and "La Vie En Rose."

Louis was born in a section of New Orleans that was so rough it was dubbed "The Battlefield." After his father left, he was forced to drop out of school so he could collect junk and deliver coal to help support his family.

As a youth, Louis was arrested when he shot his stepfather's gun in the air during a party. The police confined him to a boys' home as a punishment. There, he learned to play the cornet and discovered his passion for music.

In 1914, horn player Joe *"King Oliver"* Louis taught Satch and let him play in his place. This earned him a gig with the finest band in town, Kid Ory's. Louis rose to fame in the 1920s for his vocal and trumpet mastery.

Although he started as a jazz performer, he was hailed as a virtuoso for his rare talent and stage presence. His swinging sounds and acting helped the Grammy Hall of Fame winning singer capture the hearts of his generation and beyond.

VOTE

ROSA PARKS

7053

DAILY NEWS

SEGREGATION

FEBRUARY 4, 1913 ~ OCTOBER 24, 2005 TUSKEGEE, ALABAMA USA

CIVIL RIGHTS ACTIVIST Rosa Parks refused to give up her bus seat to a white passenger and ignited the Montgomery Bus Boycott.

A rebel with a cause, Rosa was born to a carpenter and a teacher in Alabama. When she was two, she moved to her grandparents' farm. Her grandparents were former slaves who lived in Pine Level, a town that separated people based on their skin color.

Growing up, Rosa heard the Ku Klux Klan, a group that promotes hate, ride by her home at night. She feared that her home would be burned down. Despite the risks, Rosa fought back when white children bullied her.

In 1955, Rosa refused to give up her seat in the "colored section" of a city bus to a white person after the "whites only" section was full. When asked if she stayed seated because she was tired, Rosa said, *"The only tired I was, was tired of giving in."*

She was arrested, and black people all over the city stopped using the buses in protest. This forced the city of Montgomery to end segregation on public buses.

Rosa was an activist for the rest of her life and supported many causes. The U.S. Congress named her "the mother of the freedom movement" and her legacy lives on in all who refuse to obey unfair rules that hurt and divide people today.

NAOMI ★ CAMPBELL

MAY 22, 1970 STREATHAM, LONDON UNITED KINGDOM

SUPERMODEL and **ACTRESS** Naomi Campbell was the first black woman on the cover of French Vogue.

Naomi took the spotlight at an early age. She enrolled in stage school at three, and made her TV debut in the video for Bob Marley's reggae anthem "Is This Love" at age seven.

Naomi was raised by her mother, a professional dancer of Jamaican-Chinese descent. She traveled to Italy, where her mother worked, and lived with relatives while she was on tour.

Back in England, she studied ballet at the Italia Conti Academy. Aged 15, Naomi was spotted by the head of a modeling agency while shopping. She appeared on the cover of British *Elle* before her 16th birthday.

Naomi became the first black woman to be featured on the covers of French and British *Vogue*, and *Time*. Her catwalk stride earned her spot as a supermodel for the world's top designers. Although she faced discrimination in a mostly-white industry, Naomi persisted. Saying, *"I will not shut up"* Naomi speaks out against racism in fashion to help make the field more diverse.

SAMUEL COLERIDGE-TAYLOR

AUG. 15, 1875 – SEPT. 1, 1912
HOLBORN, LONDON·ENGLAND

Samuel Coleridge-Taylor was a mixed-race English COMPOSER, known as the "African Mahler."

Samuel started playing the violin aged five. Inspired by a professional musician uncle, the young violinist joined a church choir and developed his skills.

Aged 15, Samuel went to the Royal College of Music, London. During college, he fell in love with his classmate Jessie. Although her parents opposed their relationship because of Samuel's heritage, they married and had a son named Hiawatha.

Samuel combined traditional tunes and concert music in his classical pieces. In 1898, the successful première of his masterpiece *"Hiawatha's Wedding Feast"* established him as a celebrated musician. Despite suffering injustices, he was invited to the White House by President Roosevelt, which was very rare for a person of color at that time. In 1910, he defied discrimination again by conducting white orchestras while on tour in the U.S.

Although Samuel's career ended when he passed away aged 37, he paved the way for black classical artists for generations to come.

CHAMP

G.O.A.T.

MUHAMMAD ★ ALI ★

(born CASSIUS MARCELLUS CLAY, JR.)

JANUARY 17, 1942 – JUNE 3, 2016 · LOUISVILLE, KY · USA

Muhammad Ali was a world-renowned heavyweight champion **BOXER**, famous for his unstoppable work ethic.

When Cassius was 12, someone stole his bicycle. He told Joe Martin, a police officer, he was going to beat up the person who took his bike. Mr. Martin told Cassius that he needed to learn how to fight correctly, and taught him how to box.

His ability to move faster than other fighters his size helped him win 100 out of 105 fights. In 1960,

his powerful punches took him to Italy to win the Olympic gold. Cassius' victory in Rome led to a professional boxing career. As he prepared for a fight, he pledged to *"Float like a butterfly and sting like a bee."* His jibe turned into his badge of honor when he became the heavyweight champion of the world. Soon after, he converted to Islam and changed his name to Muhammad Ali.

In 1981, Muhammad hung up his boxing gloves. In the years that followed, the Presidential Medal of Freedom winner helped the United Nations provide food, medicine, clothing, and education to people in need.

Shirley Chisholm

NOVEMBER 30, 1924 – JANUARY 1, 2005
BROOKLYN, NEW YORK·USA

FOR PRES

c72

Shirley Chisholm was the first African-American CONGRESSWOMAN in the U.S.

Shirley began her life as the first of four daughters born to immigrant parents. At five, she sailed to Barbados to live on her grandmother's farm, while her parents worked in New York. She went to a one-room schoolhouse with strict teachers who helped her refine her speaking and writing talent.

In 1939, Shirley returned to Brooklyn. At Brooklyn College, a professor noticed her "quick mind and debating skills" and urged her to pursue politics. She joined the debate team and started her own club after another group barred blacks.

Shirley never asked for permission to be included. She took her rightful place and paved the way for others. She said, *"If they don't give you a seat at the table, bring a folding chair."*

Her drive led Shirley to become the first African-American candidate to run for president in 1972. In 2015, President Obama named her a recipient of the Presidential Medal of Freedom.

STEVE McQUEEN

OCT 9, 1969
LONDON, ENGLAND UK

Steve McQueen is a British FILM DIRECTOR, visual artist, screenwriter, and producer.

In 1969, Steven was born in London to working-class parents from Trinidad and Grenada. Aged five, he showed artistic promise when Shepherd's Bush Library displayed a drawing he made of his family.

But Steve felt the impact of injustice early on. A gifted artist at age 13, he was disappointed that some students were given special privileges and others were pushed into manual labor roles. Sad about his school's lack of support, drawing became Steve's escape. He longed for creative black role models and struggled with his grades.

Steve's father wanted him to study a trade, but his artistic talent gained him admission into Chelsea College of Arts and later, to film school.

Steve went on to direct a film based on *12 Years A Slave*, a historic memoir about a free African-American who was kidnapped and sold into captivity. His movie earned him an Academy Award and raised awareness about the horrors of slavery. In 2014, he dedicated his prize to people impacted by slavery and declared, *"Everyone deserves not just to survive, but to live."*

ZADIE SMITH

**OCTOBER 29, 1975
LONDON,
ENGLAND · UK**

WHITE TEETH

Zadie Smith is a **PRIZE-WINNING NOVELIST**, essayist, and short story writer.

Born Sadie, Smith was raised by a Jamaican mother and an English father in London. A studious and creative kid, she spent her childhood developing her passion for tap dancing and musical theater.

Aged 14, Sadie changed her name to "Zadie." Inspired by her favorite writer, Vladimir Nabokov, she began shaping her literary voice.

Zadie went to study at the prestigious University of Cambridge. While there, the aspiring author worked as a jazz singer, and published short stories in a collection that caught the attention of a publisher. Zadie wrote her first novel, *White Teeth*, in her final year at university. The book, about three diverse families in modern-day London, was published to critical acclaim. It paved the way for her career as an award-winning author and writing professor.

When asked for writing advice, Zadie said: *"When still a child, make sure you read a lot of books. Spend more time doing this than anything else."*

USAIN BOLT

AUGUST 21, 1986
SHERWOOD CONTENT, JAMAICA

Usain Bolt is a **WORLD-RECORD BREAKING SPRINTER** and the fastest human alive.

Before eight-time Olympic champion Usain St Leo Bolt became known as the "lightning bolt," he was born to grocery store owners in the small town of Sherwood Content, Jamaica. When Usain and his siblings weren't helping at the store, they followed their athletic parents' footsteps by running, playing cricket, and playing football.

When Bolt began to outpace his mother and father aged 10, they supported him by growing yams to fortify his body. Powered by a yam-fueled Jamaican diet and a zest for sports, Bolt began outrunning his classmates.

By the time he was 12, he had competed in the annual national primary school's meet for the Trelawney parish, and won the title as his school's fastest 100-meter sprinter. He rose to international prominence when his 200-meter victory made him the youngest World-Junior gold medalist.

Despite his speed and natural talent, Bolt struggled with repeated injuries related to a curve in his spine during his youth. As he grew older, he learned how to beat scoliosis as fiercely as he does his competitors—by keeping his back and core strong.

Although Bolt respects great athletes who paved the way, he proudly claims his current position as the fastest man alive, saying *"A lot of legends have come before me, but this is my time."*

WANGARI MAATHAI

APRIL 1, 1940–SEPT. 25, 2011
NYERI DISTRICT, KENYA

MAMA MITI

Wangari Maathai was a Kenyan **ENVIRONMENTAL ACTIVIST** and Nobel Peace Prize laureate.

Wangari grew up on a farm in the Kenyan highlands. Her family lived among lush fruit trees and flowing rivers. She went to school when she was eight, even though it was rare for girls at the time. Early on, she became curious about how and why living things grow.

Later, she went to college in the U.S. where she became inspired by the civil rights movement. When Wangari returned home, she was shocked to discover that many of her beloved trees had been cut down by builders. She found that the earth was dry due to the lack of shade, and crops were damaged. So she started the "Green Belt Movement" to plant new forests in Kenya.

Wangari led the charge to plant over 30 million trees and offer 30,000 women skills to build a better life. She said *"It's the little things citizens do. That's what will make the difference. My little thing is planting trees."*

Despite her death in 2011, the seeds she planted by standing up for nature continue to grow worldwide.

Mae Jemison

OCTOBER 17, 1956 • DECATUR, ALABAMA • USA

ASTRONAUT Dr. Mae C. Jemison was the first African-American woman to travel in space.

Mae set her sights on the stars early on. She was a curious child raised by a carpenter and a teacher in Alabama and Chicago. When she wasn't hard at work studying, she was dancing, acting in plays, and reading about science.

Mae was fascinated by astronomy and the workings of the human body. Her childhood interest in science and medicine led her to study biochemical engineering at Stanford University, and later to become a doctor for the Peace Corps in Sierra Leone and Liberia.

Mae said *"I always knew I'd go to space,"* and she pursued this lifelong dream when she returned to the U.S. She applied for NASA's astronaut training program and became the first African-American woman in their space program in 1987. In 1992, she soared to even higher heights as the first African-American woman to travel into space.

55

ACTIVIST W.E.B. Du Bois co-founded the National Association for the Advancement of Colored People.

William grew up in Great Barrington, a community with few black residents in Massachusetts. His father left the family when William was a child.

Aged 16, his mother passed away, leaving William out in the world on his own. In the face of hardship, William became the first black student to graduate from his high school. He said *"Education and work are the levers to uplift a people."*

In 1885, William went to study at Fisk University in Tennessee. He enjoyed having more access to black culture at Fisk, but his experiences with discrimination led him to examine the roots of racism. His studies inspired him to become an activist.

William, now known as "W.E.B.," went on to become one of the leading black voices of the 20th century, and co-founded the National Association for the Advancement of Colored People, a multiracial civil rights group that still advances justice today.

W.E.B. Du BOIS
FEBRUARY 23, 1868 – AUGUST 27, 1963
GREAT BARRINGTON, MASSACHUSETTS
USA

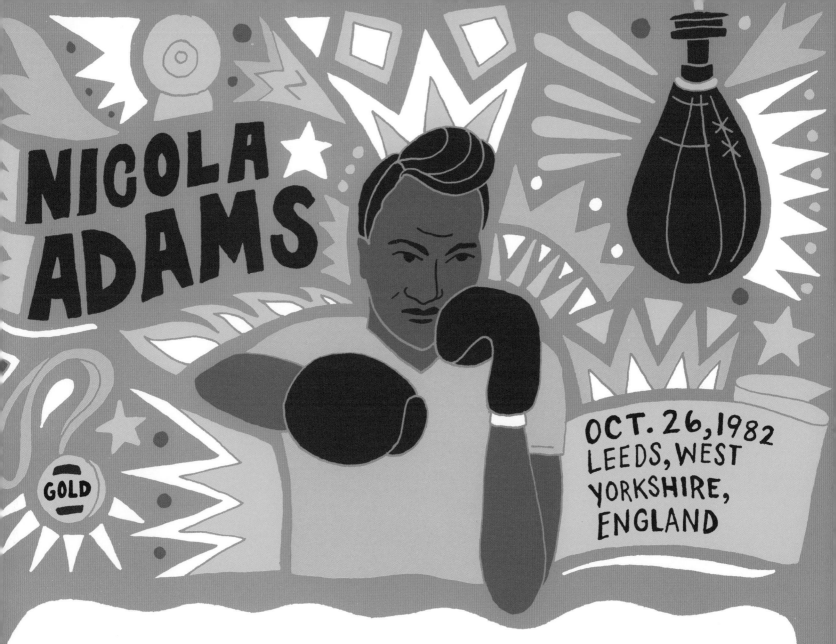

NICOLA ADAMS

OCT. 26, 1982
LEEDS, WEST
YORKSHIRE,
ENGLAND

GOLD

Nicola Adams is a **PROFESSIONAL BOXER** from Britain. She is the first woman to win an Olympic boxing title and holds multiple gold medals.

Nicola has been beating the odds since childhood. She grew up in a rough neighborhood in Leeds, where she found comfort watching videos of boxing greats like Muhammad Ali with her father. Nicola became inspired by Ali's graceful and quick moves and decided that she wanted to be a prize-fighter like him.

Despite being sick with asthma and allergies, she told her mother that she would win a gold medal for

her fighting skills—years before women's boxing became an Olympic sport. At 12, she followed her mother to the gym because her babysitter didn't show up. There, she discovered a children's boxing class and became hooked on sparring.

Britain's most decorated fighter won her first match aged 13, despite a lack of opportunities for female boxers. She became the first female to win an Olympic boxing title after she won the 2012 Olympic gold medal in the women's flyweight division. She said, *"I just always wanted to win. I don't think about losing until it happens."*

SERENA WILLIAMS
SEPTEMBER 26, 1981
SAGINAW, MICHIGAN · USA

& VENUS WILLIAMS
JUNE 17, 1980
LYNWOOD, CALIFORNIA · USA

Serena Williams and her sister Venus Williams are considered two of the best women's **TENNIS PLAYERS** in history.

The Williams Sisters are two of Richard Williams and Oracene Price's five daughters. While they are most famous for being two of the best athletes of all time, their bond as sisters surpasses their strength. Serena said, *"Family's first, and that's what matters most. We realize that our love goes deeper than the tennis game."*

Their father Richard, a former sharecropper from Louisiana, dreamed that his daughters would become tennis champions. He studied books and instructional videos to help teach them how to play by the time they were three. His coaching paid off. At four, Serena won her first tournament.

When the girls were kids, their family moved to a white stucco house in a tough community in Compton, California. Their father used their harsh surroundings to motivate them to study and work hard.

With his support, the girls sometimes practiced tennis on courts with dents and missing nets for two-hours or more each day. They trained so hard that they broke racket strings from hitting up to 500 balls with force. They developed powerful serves in the process.

Tennis became their refuge from the violence that riddled their community, and it elevated them to the world's stage when they rose to fame in the 1990s. Despite their unmatched talent, they faced criticism and exclusion due to racism and their unique style. They debuted within a year of each other as professional players, and have been making waves on and off the court as sportswomen and helpers for causes close to their hearts.

MISTY COPELAND

SEPTEMBER 10, 1982
KANSAS CITY, MO · USA

Misty Copeland was the first African-American ballerina to be appointed as a PRINCIPAL DANCER for the American Ballet Theatre, one of the leading ballet companies in the United States.

Misty has always lived her life in fluid and constant motion. Frequent moves and conflict at home rocked her childhood, but she kept going.

After sleeping on the floors of motels with her five siblings, and regularly enduring hunger, Misty moved to California. Despite her harsh upbringing, participating in dance classes at her new school became a source of peace. She said, *"Finding ballet was like finding a missing piece of myself."*

While studying under ballet instructor Cindy Bradley, Misty found inspiration in the story and work of gymnast Nadia Comaneci and created routines to the music of singer Mariah Carey. Her endless drive led her to serve as the captain of her middle school's drill team. Later, it earned her a spot on the American Ballet Theatre's studio company and corps de ballet.

In 2015, Misty became the first African-American principal dancer in the company's history. Her spry agility in performances of *The Firebird* and *The Nutcracker* gained global attention due to her unique flair. This cemented her position as one of the few black performers at the highest levels of classical dance. *Time* magazine named her one of the "100 Most Influential People" for her pioneering work and her outspokenness about diversity in the dance world.

HALL of FAME

Who will you choose to read about today? Turn to the page numbers below to find them.

28 MAURICE ASHLEY

29 ALEXANDRE DUMAS

30 MARTIN LUTHER KING, JR.

32 MAYA ANGELOU

33 NINA SIMONE

34 SIMONE BILES

36 STEVIE WONDER

38 ESPERANZA SPALDING

39 SIDNEY POITIER

40 OPRAH WINFREY

41 PELÉ

42 NELSON MANDELA

44 LOUIS ARMSTRONG

45 ROSA PARKS

46 NAOMI CAMPBELL

47 SAMUEL COLERIDGE-TAYLOR

48 MUHAMMAD ALI

49 SHIRLEY CHISHOLM

50 STEVE McQUEEN

51 ZADIE SMITH

52 USAIN BOLT

54 WANGARI MAATHAI

55 MAE JEMISON

56 W.E.B. DU BOIS

57 NICOLA ADAMS

58 SERENA WILLIAMS

58 VENUS WILLIAMS

60 MISTY COPELAND

GLOSSARY

Activist: A person who campaigns for changes
Civil rights: The rights every human has to be free and equal
Culture: The arts and ideas of a group of people
Discrimination: Unfair treatment of people based on race, age, or gender
Equality: Being equal in rights and opportunities
Segregation: Separating people into different groups based on skin color

For Isa, may you be inspired and empowered to forever live out your dreams.—A.P.
For Mom, Dad, my ancestors, and the next generation. I am because you are.—J.W.

Inspiring | Educating | Creating | Entertaining

Brimming with creative inspiration, how-to projects, and useful information to enrich your everyday life, Quarto Knows is a favorite destination for those pursuing their interests and passions. Visit our site and dig deeper with our books into your area of interest: Quarto Creates, Quarto Cooks, Quarto Homes, Quarto Lives, Quarto Drives, Quarto Explores, Quarto Gifts, or Quarto Kids.

Young, Gifted and Black © 2018 Quarto Publishing plc.
Text © 2018 Jamia Wilson.
Illustrations © 2018 Andrea Pippins.
Photo credits pp 62—63 © Alamy Stock Photo.

First Published in 2018 by Wide Eyed Editions, an imprint of The Quarto Group.
400 First Avenue North, Suite 400, Minneapolis, MN 55401, USA.
T (0)20 7700 6700 F (0)20 7700 8066 **www.QuartoKnows.com**

The right of Andrea Pippins to be identified as the illustrator and Jamia Wilson to be identified as the author of this work has been asserted by them in accordance with the Copyright, Designs and Patents Act, 1988 (United Kingdom).

A catalogue record for this book is available from the British Library.

ISBN 978-1-78603-158-7

The illustrations were created in ink and colored digitally
Set in Futura, Buttacup Lettering, and Azaelia

Published by Jenny Broom • Designed by Karissa Santos
Edited by Katy Flint • Production by Jenny Cundill

Manufactured in Guangdong, China [CC] in 112017

9 8 7 6 5 4 3 2 1